Live Coverage

Also by Priscila Uppal

Poetry
How to Draw Blood from a Stone
Confessions of a Fertility Expert
Pretending to Die

Novel
The Divine Economy of Salvation

Non-fiction
Uncommon Ground: A Celebration of Matt Cohen,
co-edited with Graeme Gibson, Wayne
Grady, and Dennis Lee

LIVE COVERAGE

Priscila Uppal

Exile Editions

TORONTO
2003

National Library of Canada Cataloguing in Publication

Uppal, Priscila
  Live coverage / Priscila Uppal.
Poems.
ISBN 1-55096-571-9
  I. Title.
PS8591.P62L49 2003   C811'.54   C2003-904850-0

This edition is published by Exile Editions Limited,
20 Dale Avenue, Toronto, Ontario, Canada   M4W 1K4

Sales Distribution:
McArthur & Company c/o Harper Collins
1995 Markham Road, Toronto, ON   M1B 5M8
toll free: 1 800 387 0117
(fax) 1 800 668 5788

Composition and Cover Design by TIM HANNA
Cover painting "L'OMBRELLE" BY LEONOR FINI.
Author Photograph by CHRISTOPHER DODA
Printed and Bound at TRANSCONTINENTAL PRINTING

The publisher wishes to acknowledge
the assistance toward publication of
the Canada Council and the Ontario Arts Council.

THE CANADA COUNCIL   LE CONSEIL DES ARTS
FOR THE ARTS   DU CANADA
SINCE 1957   DEPUIS 1957

ONTARIO ARTS COUNCIL
CONSEIL DES ARTS DE L'ONTARIO

ISBN 1-55096-571-9
Printed in Canada

for Athena, who commanded Stop Now

Oh for shame, how the mortals put the blame upon us
gods, for they say evils come from us, but it is they, rather,
who by their own recklessness win sorrow beyond what is given.

Film at Eleven Film at Eleven Film at Eleven Film at Eleven Film at Eleven Film at Eleven

We shall not tolerate
terrorists, cried
Odysseus.

Then the men were
gone. Gone for
twenty years.

The women wept.
The children cheered.
We pinned ribbons

to our chests
lest we forget.
Knowing it true.

War is horrible,
horrible. Unless
fought for you.

But if you are one among many who live in this country, three times blessed are you father and

Because blood is an *idea*, someone always wants to tamper with it.
Forgetting it the centre of horror stories.
The ultimate excuse for all sorts of bad behavior.

If one could measure the word with the actual substance,
our family trees would be soaked.
Our myths would stink
like the hottest trash.

As eventually:

the line is cut: be it silently
or violently.

Be it by scientists with silver
test tubes
and end results.

Be it by cutting off a woman's tongue
so she cannot utter
her father's name.

the lady your mother, and three times blessed your brothers too, and I know their spirits are

Angry. More than any first principles he knows that he is
angry, and circles the room like a magnet at the poles, dirt
on his hinges. He wipes it off and keeps circling, not caring
what sticks, what will never come away.

My father is a war-god. And he is worth worshipping.
I have done so for decades, though he does not know this. Though
he spins his wheels until dizzy and tired and ill.

Do you sense the harsh tide rising? Spitting fish straight
out of the sea? Those wading by the shores face-down on the sands?

Can you blame him? The goddesses took his legs and ran away.
His children do not know where to find them. Everywhere he turns
there are traps and riddles and strangely familiar faces with one eye.

When the first bomb made impact a handful of men were up in space. They witnessed a puff of smoke, a minor fire, nothing of the plane. They had just begun floating in orbit. *Did you see where?* one asked another. *Someplace in the West. If it's important, we'll hear about it.* And they kept circling, circling their beloved sky. *I could die here,* the youngest said. *Not on my shift,* laughed the captain. Tower Two made an orange dot on the screen. The radio bleeped. *All these years, I've never seen one,* was announced before the silence.

Massacre/As for that other one, I will not tell you the whole story whether he lives or has died.

at least one thousand heads of households will be out of work.
Imagine the calamity, the threat to the economy. Sure,

I understand no one thinks it will happen, especially after Y2K. But
I'm rarely shocked by shock anymore. Cannibalism, Anti-Semitism,
Genocide. I used to blow up with grief. Used

to think I'd somehow got the facts wrong. Cambodia, Rwanda,
Bosnia, Persian Gulf, sounded so far away
unthinkable until entering my vocabulary

on TV, the weeklies, crosswords. Clincher
in the puzzle, question on *Jeopardy!*: Category: "Over" the Rainbow,
Over in quotation marks, we know what that means:

Answer: Icy phrase: A response to responsibility.

If it does though, there'll be explaining to do. Statistics to quote.
Videos and dramatic recreations to analyze. Who let the
devils wear parkas and operate snow blowers?

Who allowed their factories to shut down, children go hungry,
crops dry out, to find us
unprotected, unprepared?

It is bad to babble emptily/U.S. researchers using the newly published human gene map said

Men leapt off mountains
gagged and blindfolded.
Villages rose and died in a word.
Mother kept unmentionables in a jar.

The mandolin
served the government. Dancing
was characteristic
of dusk. Sex scuttled in the form
of misshapen animals.

Marriage was an institution
of prince-makers.
Adultery a stifled burp.
Seafaring a common,
terminal activity.
Life lugged itself to the four corners.

Father owned his body
and his soul.
Refused to let the fates sell
him up the river
for a television appearance
and a million dollars,

for nothing less
than absolute immortality.

this week they had identified 19 genetic regions linked with depression/What man's thrall are

Ledger lives.
Record the recordable.
The sun is not admissible evidence.
Neither is your pain.

Women fall in love
and men fall
in graves.
Flowers pander to the masses.

Glory, glory.
Alleluia.
Be free.
Be good.
God Bless You.

My kingdom
for a horse.
A hand.
A shot of penicillin.

Damned
if you do.
Damned
if you

you? Whose orchard are you laboring?/Show Trials are Not the Solution to Saddam's Heinous

Polls show the majority of contributing citizens
believe in the extermination of their fellow men
when they pose a clear and present danger but few are willing
to carry out the sentence.

They send representatives known as diplomats.

Pontius Pilate was a diplomat too.
No one since has washed his hands with such supple skill.

He knew the way down the mountain
was mapped out
by opinion.

No rails

to catch a stray lamb's fall.

Reign/Dreams are things hard to interpret, hopeless to puzzle out, and people find that not all of

Since the bombs have gone off,
I've been daydreaming in red. Red faces, red carpets,
red painted houses, red washed walls. At first, it was disturbing,
this world of blood and fire, the final hour. But then
you see, then, it made sense. We were never
anything but red. Red eyes, red teeth, red hair. The world
is red. Look at how we try to hide it with skin! If given
the chance to begin again, I say we accept.
I say we rip open our chests
and live in red
like the wounds the fatal wounds
we are.

Forensics has a duty: tell us
which bones were broken, fractured, crushed, taken

how the perpetrator operated: from imprints
of bruises and grass samples
it is ascertainable
the fatal blow was dealt at ten past the hour
in the thicket behind the baseball diamond:
he penetrated her three times, twice while
she was unconscious. Don't

omit the analysis of his semen, or his violent juvenile
history, or the print mark her teeth made when she pierced
the side of his armpit. Scratches on his chin took
two weeks to heal.

The public takes pity if not her killer.
She fought to get away, the detectives
are sure of it, and the ex-boyfriend-in-question dropped
as a suspect. His family firm all along he was

incapable of such atrocity: girls extracted from ditches
and ducts, suitcases and hotel rooms, basement apartments,
in the walls chopped

into blocks, strangled with their own hair, choking
on feces. Give us every detail. We must know
how her eyes blinked in unison
with the slap of the whip how she cried
Momma, Momma until losing
her head, vomit on her skirt, blood
on her neck, pointed objects up her cunt
so that initially it was believed
she'd been crucified.

the democratic process, confident the United States would realize it had made what he says is a

We need to know, those who love her.
Sealed and bagged. Exhibit A. You cannot forsake us
to the dark. This street filled with sewage, you bet there's a stench,

but we're fighters, tough, and the pain
bearable if you trust
there will be an end. Prosecution,
the promise is, brings peace.

mistake and release his son/And once the spirit has left the white bones, all the rest of the body

That's what the Greeks called her.
Terrified: those eyes alone
enough to drill holes
in your belly and let the sustenance spill out.

No worse crime than inhospitality in *The Odyssey*.
Punishable by death, or a family
rampage. Take your pick.

Wine and sweet meats. This was the way to win
wars and women. A bed for the night
and a harp player
to rest your head against and weep.

Grief was out in the open. Men bawled
like babies. Women scolded them, *Get back out there
you cowards, and stop fussing.*

But somewhere along the line (have we inherited sea-
sickness?) no goddess wants to keep
her roast or pastries down.

She speed skates to the river
bones sharp as spears and
breasts bound with tape.
A feast the furthest thing
from her mind.

is made subject to the fire's stong fury, but the soul flitters out/Floods caused by pounding mon-

A hero, she set out. For the far land she read about in one of her books buckled up like children in her boat. No help from the gods of weather, fifteen years it took to make it ashore. This I can survive, she sang. Bore down upon the sand, cut her toes on a beer can. This I can survive, she sang again. Then appeared men in potato-sack togas and driving TransAms. I come bearing books, she said, from Paradise. That's nice, they replied, kicked her in the stomach, then forced seeds inside. This I can survive, she cried. This I can survive.

The books, bloated and torn, floated along the bank. A plague visited the land. The men suited up in plastic masks, she in her straw coat. This I can survive, she said. I will make it to Paradise. And they laughed again and threw her down, then decided she wasn't worth it. She was getting old anyway. So she clawed her way back up the hole and found her little boat and her books.

But she could not remember why she was so fond of books when they could not eat, or fight, or scream. This I can survive, she said again. Then she drank the sea.

soon rains have left some 77 people dead in Bangladesh and India and marooned almost two

your instincts are true. Oceans blue
at the bottom. Volcanoes cough
ash. Money grabbers in the temple
were right. We are not biblical, but carbon
dated, and diamonds, stones of little value.

Swim across the English Channel.
Fly around the world.
Buy a rocket and hurtle into space.

This was meant to happen
(dreams broke free, broke free
into the stratosphere, the hard shells
of our skulls).

Our machines plan no revolt.
The elements remain in place.
Engineers oil the gears of this planet
and we crack our backs in our beds

(and speaking of beds)

before science made it official
I was already
giving birth
to other people's babies.

million/Poor fools, and they had not yet realized how over all of them the terms of death were

Three millennia ago there was no such thing as
a stapler, but a recent archaeological dig
revealed a tool likened to a stapler which may
have been utilized for a stapler-like purpose although
there was no such thing as paper, only paperish
substances which enabled transmission
of text in such and such a manner as
we now may think of paper.

Ten millennia ago there may or may not have been families
in our sense of the word, though dating
is far from an exact science we can rightly
conjecture that where there are babies
there requires a structure similar
to our understanding of family, possibly
extended family, but we musn't impose
our contemporary conceptions upon the elusive
past, even if we are almost unfailingly sure
primitive cultures thought about
the past and/or babies.

Forty millennia ago there may not have been evidence
to explain the bubbling on the surface
like the reaction of soda
to vinegar although sodium or hydrogen
wouldn't have mixed,
though they would have intuitively collided
into molecules that wouldn't necessarily
have acted like molecules but in a fashion
or order random and wild and unnamed
about to become originals while we
must console ourselves with archetype,
our dreamers, our cataclysmic clairvoyants.

What bliss was ignorance.

Tribe leader
William Oltetia expressed
extreme sadness
when informed
of the historical happenings
on September 7th (the date
did not translate)
in June of 2002.

Relief soon followed.
Masai had been spared.

Fourteen cows
shipped to
the United States,
to go along with
Canadian soldiers
and British pounds.

Blessed by the tribe,
the gift will land
in Washington
by plane
on the eve of June 5[th]2002.

Yet more gods to consume.

how much artery-clogging trans-fats the products contain/Nobody really knows his own

After being absent for twenty years
disguising one's self in front of your father
for the purpose of play
is the curse

of old age. Regardless of whether
you bring along victuals
and a personal maid,

people like to play tricks on eyes,
on history, on the way
you know things happen.

Despite the fight, the good
intentions, the treasures,
and glorious kills
you will end your life

as you ended your father's.
Though he massacred
all the young minds and bodies
of his country

to see you safe, Telemachos
will show you as much mercy
as the gods

when they've already
bartered your life away.

In Charon's waiting room you can question
the receptionist until you're blue in the face
but no one will answer. She speaks
the language of form:

reason for visit, time since last visit,
referrals, family history, insurance.

Plastic plants grace the dock
and unclaimed oars. The scale is temporarily
out of order. The *Sounds of the Rainforest*
tape plays in a loop.

You were supposed to be diagnosed hours ago.

You stare at others, playing cards
or forgetting, wondering what they've got
to be cresting here, if it's catching.
Fold hands in front, keep
eyes low and mumble.

There is only one magazine, which you've already read.

winds all burst out/If you want a happy young reader, you need to buy age-appropriate

Woman led to believe man
most important to woman.
Baby most important to man.

Woman cooks.
Man eats.
Baby eats.

Woman takes time off.
Man goes away on business.
Woman has baby and no man.

Man does not return.
If man does return he brings new woman.
A neighbour tells her.

Man wakes with bullet in his chest.
Baby wakes with bullet in his chest.
Woman goes to sleep with bullet in her head.

Read your classics.

books/Whose eyes can follow the movement of a god, passing from place to place, unless the god

Virginia would like to know. Marriage
was never her strong point either, though she managed
to negotiate a room and a publishing house
out of the deal.

She wants to be released from the dinner drinks
circling in the parlours. The dirty jukebox
dancing halls. Umbrellas,
and jokes

no one gets when they're sober. *I never
frightened a fly*, she testifies

by force of The Big Man, transcripts
in triplicate to sign. *It was just
a rumour, a silly play a woman
would never have written (she'd have
killed the child herself)*. Swear.

Fear is on a platter
for your consumption. When dead
there's no more hunger. Bodies free
from longing and colours unreachable. Nothing
but women rising out of the sea
could scare me so.

On Wednesday afternoon
after a routine check-up
of aquarium D

the vet on call
returned to her lunch room
and told her superiors
and later the media
the definite pregnancy
of Dolphin generation #4
the one the children named Soda
for her pop-can-like spray.

A male dolphin
had not entered her
tank in over a year.

Workers let out a cheer.
Biologists puzzled over the new puzzle.
Believers believed
and guards took on the burden
of guarding.

After three days
the public forgot
Soda, went back to tabloid
critters with pig ears and horse
tails, living proof
of aliens and Elvis.

When the manager
took out an announcement in the paper
on the blessed day,
he was shocked to relay
not a single person had tried to kill her.

contraceptive options and a new era of birth control/Charybdis sucks down the black water.

If there is no continuing city, then there is no continuing garden.
Peter V. Marinelli

Take your place under the listless leaves.
The city is raised, like Cain, for tough
dealings.

Watch the struggle in the sewers. Seedlings swim
to subways, clog up the
system.

Watch blossoms get abducted, then thrown
out with the trash. Shepherds
take to the bridges.

Water's not free, child.
Get your own.

If sickness persists, call authorities,
paint red or pink targets
on trunks, ropes around necks.

The larger body
will absorb it.

Don't ever sing
or lay laurels.

This isn't Arcadia.

We won't replant with the next government grant.

We'll sign up
for self-defense
lessons instead.

For three times a day she flows it up, and three times she sucks it terribly down; may you not be

Mother off the wagon again, locked
in her room with the lights curtailed and fingers
mummified. She wears the slash of lightning
in her limbs and patterns of chisel across
her eyelids. Two

whole days she refuses to come out for air
or tea or lemonade. She can live off fear and pity,
the children think, no strength to move today,
another cancelled appointment at the dentist's
or doctor's. Do

the survey in the cellar of the magazine. Does she manifest
symptoms: lack of sleep, shakes, obsessive mania. Children
prepare beds and phone calls, apologies
and her reddest robe. The walls
crochet a net thick as her mother's thighs
when she said, *You*

think you're as talented as me? Well
you'll soon see. Cut her webs, smashed the awards,
drove her father mad, the young ladies into tunnels.
But that wasn't enough. She needed to be black.
Black and blue. With many more eyes to boot.

there when she sucks down water, for not even the Earthshaker could rescue you out of that

When mother moved out and took the television with her, father had to resort to the fancies of his youth. He hopped on one leg with such style I could not catch him, tied knots with several varieties of string, and stole colouring books from the supermarket, shading all in red. This last one had us puzzled. *Father*, my brother said, *surely there are other colours.* *The television is gone*, my father replied. *And so is mother. She is dead*, he said. *She is red, red, red.*

He stopped hopping and tying and eventually colouring. But that took a long time. Four winters to be exact before we could tear down the wall-paper of red dogs and red houses, whole red scenes from the latest Disney picture. By then we had a television and a new mother but no one watched either.

One day father gathered my brother and me on the carpet before him, cross-legged in the traditional manner, cut his nails into the shapes of animals and threw them on the floor. *We are switching religions*, he said proudly. *You are Noah and his wife. Save me.*

"Send back the subpoena
to the girl on the corner who suffered
a brain haemorrhage
contemplating the city's misuse
of water plant revenue
and the subsequent deaths of citizens
of her planet
Earth, where she hoped to
work as an elementary
school teacher but filled
out the wrong forms
and was placed
in the line of those tested positive
for Frequent Thoughts Against
the Ruling Province
and failed miserably
to attribute pain, disease, poverty
to those who deserve it.

Please tell her
I will give her a dollar
(if that's what she wants)
when she gets
off her high horse,
brushes her hair,
and starts working off
her parents' debt."

(Instructions: Do not linger
when you hand over the envelope.
Pretend you are late
for a conference or the streetcar.
Above all, do not touch.)

generous/Vacations can bring out the best and the worst in people. Although everyone may be

About the young girl in the square
in Zagreb at a table with her father
watching the band play while you ate lunch.

Sequestered on her father's knee,
tapping a beat with clumsy hands, you
watched with weariness, knowing the beer glass
would soon topple.

The man scolded her and though the day was sunny
she bent her head under the umbrella, tears
rolling down without reserve, mixing with the gold
water. Knowing she did wrong.

You won't admit that you know
why that girl's tender cry hasn't left you since, though
you went to witness the destruction in Dubrovnic, your grand-
mother's ransacked village, and recent memorials
to remind tourists of landmines. From the Dalmatian Coast

and across the border to Hungary, her orphan eyes peeked from
stone, her tears fell like a good Catholic's over the entire seaboard
and good times never seemed as good as she sat beside you
settling her hand in yours like decade-worn dust.

You let go of the grammar lessons, numerous
declensions to distinguish subject from object you had trouble
memorizing, the old friends and professional contacts who offered
you wine and a corner of an apartment to rest while they talked in circles.

You let go of finding your past self in archways and lines of poetry
or the rotating bands in the square. But the girl who disappointed her
father defects over the border—clings like the seaweed to your suit.
Yet you will not say:

intent on having fun and relaxing, things inevitably happen to interfere with that goal/This is

I know her father loves beer more than he loves her.

Isn't that *wrong?*

And yet, I will not say:

I know we love that girl's pain more than we love her.

Isn't that *wrong?*

the only consolation we wretched mortals can give, to cut our hair and let the tears roll down

Love the person not the police report.
The wrists not the weapon, the grievers
not the tears.

          The crash is not a moment
of revelation. The threat not a crux
that makes the heart race, the heart race

into your throat. Welcome words, the ordinary
orations of clerk, waitress, assistant-

to-the-one-in-charge. Discuss the nature
of violence but do not repeat. Memorize the
faces on the street, not just movie posters,

missing persons photographs. Laugh
when something is funny, not cruel. Laugh
a little more than you do.

          The home is lovely before it is broken.
Before the mistress moves in for good.
Before the children receive child-support.

Should you lick wounds do not call them
pretty. Do not compare them to flowers
or treasures from ancient stories. Do not cross

yourself for the sake of the cross. That man
I admire is not a hero because he has no legs

but because he once had legs and lives
on a street, on a continent, on a planet of legs
and gets there
gets there
in one piece.

our faces/Are You Really a Good Driver?/Hold fast. Do not strike this man with the bronze.

Blame it on your mother's looks.

Ghosts visit in the darkest hours of morning,
and only once, so you'd better listen.

Best friends can be counted on.

A step-father's love isn't worth earning anyhow.

Counsel is for the weak.

Royalty are incestuous.

Men make silly soldiers, girls elegant suicides.

Don't waste money on fine curtains.

Brothers should defend their sisters.

Be a paradox.

Every death is murder.

He is innocent./Sales of G.I. Joe action figures were up a whopping 46 percent last year says

THIS JUST IN...

Had he survived, my father would have said:
Look what happens when you put all your eggs
in one basket. When your most prized possession
is displayed in the living room. When
security is interior. When you trust
the power of intelligence
to withstand all.

Hasboro/The War God rages at all, and favors no man/New reasearch offers a surprising

In laboratories across North America:
Man and horse collide. Man and bird comply.
Insect and rodent switch significant DNA.
Scientists roar. Hedge their bets. Set new rules.
A next generation salvaged.

(The picture books did it—creatures of many names
and faces bore theories out—nature could be altered
like temperature, and density, consistency,   blood   brain
lobotomy   physiognomy   cosmic switcheroo

Rumours of babies flying off apartment rooftops
Women with hooves for feet
Lovers with webbed arms and flesh tough as cattle hide

Were made   maidens   heroes   villains
gods)

Mix sugar and water.
Vegetable and mineral.
Arm with head.

Stir until the surface settles.
Name the new genus. Preferably after a myth that trembles.
If you produce multiple eyes, do your damnedest to ensure they
remain dominant.

Call your bookie.
A creature half-lion half-giant is circling the podium.

explanation for why asthma has become a nationwide epidemic involving 5 million

Maenad
Charybdis
Cerebus
Cyclops
Centaur
Chimera
Griffen
Gorgon
Siren
Kraken
Hydra

children/Do not give any of these people your eye/The country's solicitor-general will listen to

Once man became aware of the sign
over the arches in Eden, we were done for.

Do What Thou Wilt:
Get your groove on. Get your rocks off. Just do it.

A garden is meant for eating and sleeping, and strangling
your lover in. For tampering with the ecosystem and genetic codes.

For burying your brother after you've killed him.
For raping young boys with a fleeting interest in divinity.

It's so blasé. This concern with one crime. This lady friend
who had a bit too much to drink and started shooting

her mouth off. A whiny son cut off from
the family fortune. The stuff of sit-coms and

movies of the week. It works out in the end. The spirit's
uplifted. Perseverance defies adversity. A simple, simply

feel-good story. Cover of humanity. Hollywood
ending, fortune-cookie destiny. When if we'd just read

the fine print of the contract, the alternate ending,
we'd slam the gates shut, then throw away all the goddamn keys.

concerns about their neighbourhood, which houses more than 200 sex offenders/I sent some of

Dead like the trees: the lovers who fell at the exact same moment,
mothers who wrung themselves into oak, crones and widows,
men without hope, the delirious wanderers and their ilk, fresh
petal lice and infected roots

pulled down the eyebrows, feet, burnt skin
of albinos. Trees grow on blood, on famous
last words, the promises you make and those
you have no intention of keeping
that some gullible goddesses overhear.

Stop and contemplate the trees.
They are all named because too many have done so.

Carry, stranger,
the next burden of naming:

The dead are buildings.
They have windows for eyes. Elevators for spines.

A long, long time ago, two met that loved.
It went terribly wrong, and soured.

It's a wrecking ball.
A wrecking ball.

my companions ahead, telling them to find out what men, eaters of bread, might live here/

NOW FOR YOUR FORECAST...

No longer will there be four seasons,
only two: Hot or Cold.
Me or You.

A case of West Nile virus was found in Alberta for the first time after a dead magpie

Stolen Movie Jewels Found at Murder Scene

Canada Eyes New Tests for Mad Cow

Doctor Sews Screwdriver Inside Patient's Spine

Afghan City Closes Video Game Store

Iraq After Saddam: A Guide

Let Child of Divorce Decide Wedding Protocol

Seven Deaths in Seven Days

Madonna to Appear in Gap Campaign

Bionic Ear Expands World of Hearing

Killer Asteroid Risks Downgraded

Cancer Doctors Profiting from Drugs

Lose Your Tummy by August 20th

Man Charged with Eating Net Friend

Mentally Disabled Veterans Lose Pension Case

NHL Draft: The Two Faces of Hockey

Zimbabwe Churches Apologize for Doing Too Little

Defaming Islam--One Bomb at a Time

Hero's Killer Still on the Loose

50 Euro Note is Forger's Favourite

Winnipeg Syphillis Cases Worry Authorities

Prepare for a Bar Code Revolution

Head of Medical Pot Program Resigns

Luxury Camping: Roughing it Made Easy

Masturbate and Cut Risk of Prostate Cancer

Can Bono Save the World?

tested positive for the disease/But we have killed what held the city together, the finest young

Airport Screeners Find Loaded Gun in Teddy Bear
New Chair: Turbocharged Magic Fingers
59 War Criminals Missing in Canada
Girls Drown in Alberta Irrigation Canal
Surviving in Prison
Giant Mutant Beach Bunny
Heroin Town
Mass Picket to Protest Sex Offender
Women and Meth
Crown Blindsided by Court Appearance
Burping Stars Clog Universe with Grime
Father's Nightmare Begins After Son Arrested
Queen's Plate a Big Test for Storied Bloodlines
New Hope in Peanut Allergy
UK Cops Seek Help to Find Canadian Singer's Killer
Spousal Abuse Sparks Backlash Against Victims
A Diet of Lead
Babies Store Memories at Age 2
Elvis Parts Up for Grabs
Native Healing Ceremony for Boy Shot in Eye
Mob Uses Granny's Place to Run $20M Gambling Den
Genome Survey Finds Depression Genes
It's Safe to Pack Tweezers Again
SARS May Scare Off Celebs
Welcome to the Summer of Love, Baby

men in Ithaka. It is what I could have you consider/Which Calcium Supplements Should You

They planned it. Don't forget that, after tears
are shed at the sheer sight of the horror. Children in love.
Children, clumsy. No wonder our hearts go
out to them. Tragic. Beautiful. Dead children
the most tragic, most beautiful. Yearbooks
pasted with them. And poems. Poems praising them
and their friends, how they'll be missed,
wouldn't they have become important leaders
in the community, in the world—scholarships
and babies, if only they hadn't believed
it was hopeless.

Planned at lunch hour in the lips
of notes passed in class—the love, love, unending
hatred, those who couldn't understand
or let it be and strut their stuff in front of them—
who really didn't get into each other's pants,
or lust at all—but found themselves
lumped together when lockers were assigned,
homeroom unwelcoming. Let's take
ourselves out, they said, bursting into the cafeteria.
They planned it. The guns. The notes. Yearbook
elegies. Let's take ourselves out
and a bunch of them down too.

Take?: Quiz/I am afraid of my swarm of rough suitors, whose outrageous violence goes up into

The massacre and civil suit could ostensibly
have been averted. Had the lunch ladies noticed the tension
bubble between Beowulf and Grendel

a time-out could have been ordered, a detention, the principal's
intervention by instituting a meeting, though boys
will be boys and can't save face

when mothers get involved in schoolyard feuds
and dead-beat dads scalp tickets on the sidelines. The town
cannot absorb another tragedy

of its kind, though riches were evenly distributed
among the living and his homely mug posted for one year
on telephone poles. Locals recall

he had eyes resembling a pigeon's, hid his hands in a long green
coat, and liked hamburgers. His mother loved
him unconditionally.

the iron sky/Fears, Real and Imagined, in the Life of a 10 Year-old/A curse on you, if he turns

No means No. She tried to be nice.
Tried to do as her mother taught her:
gentlemen callers ought to be treated
with respect no matter who they are.
Give them wine if they so desire, cook
a ham. They've travelled a long way
to ask for your hand. I've got ten girls
willing to testify, she told them. You better
get back to your wives. They busted
her loom, her arm, the lock on the liquor
cabinet. The prosecutor never recovered
the heads, ushered past the thousand
quilts hanging in the ancient corridor.

out to be some god from heaven. For the gods do take on all sorts of transformations, appearing

I cannot go out, she declares. Content in this day and age
groceries, magazines, medicines can come to the door.

The dust has not washed off. The white filth
on black hands as if the baker had powdered her.

Rebuild. Rebuild. The stairs are not high enough.
Must break through the clouds, reach the vertigo in the sky

that decides who will die and who will be discovered
by police, dogs, firefighters in the wreck. The chalk woman

scheduled an early appointment. A latte at the corner.
A red light. A bike courier took his sweet time.

Nine months later reporters have not left her lawn.
Mesmerized by how she's alive.

Stay hidden. Mark your windows. Memorize secret sermons.
Unscathed from the flames, swallow the Holy Spirit's tongue.

as strangers from elsewhere, and thus they range at large through the cities, watching to see

Today: the conference I've been waiting for.

Those suited to discussion of the pleasures and horrors of life will be
privy to a one-hour introductory session, twenty minutes for questions,
and complimentary refreshments immediately thereafter.
Our topic: Paradise: Centuries of Crying Over Spilt Milk.

The activities: historical reinvention, mythological continuation, divine
intervention. I've been saving up my money and slides collected
in museums. The method whereby Death is kept at a distance. Let not
a single feared symbol effect you. Snake. Apple. Lightning Bolt.
We're safe in here.

Today I'm trying not to think about where the good soldiers have
gone. The school bus crash. Or my next-door neighbour who died
of heart disease at the age of 33. The third speaker will mention
flogging, the fifth euthanasia, but it can't hurt when there's an over-
head and handouts, a woman with bifocals correcting Latin.

Avaritia, Via Negativa.
Only signs to deconstruct. A circumlocution exercise.

No one asked me to sign up. If I want out, all I need to do is leave
the room.
No one needs to make a choice. Or die.

which men keep the laws and which are violent/Two days ago, 3 1/2 year-old Jordan Arbaji

a bit like theft in the downtown core, you see
these brides flirting with chequebooks and Visa cards, a bit tentative at first
(I didn't even want a ring but he insisted, do you think a rehearsal dinner
is necessary), they are feminists after all, women who said
they'd rather die childless than trap a man and pronounce his name
in front of God and state and family (who don't much like
the choices made thus far). So there's his mother
to consider who hates the fact you live together and then the possible
babies, if babies are to be had of course, they must be born
in the next couple of years and who wants a baby to be a bastard?
It's just better, tests, surveys have shown for proper development you see,
and the metaphysical exploration of love in another dimension
(you don't want to limit the soul's expansion, do you) so
crystal is ordered and a minister summoned (you discussed a woman
minister, to make a point, but she wasn't available on the same weekend
as the jazz quartet) and the paper plate barbeque with a few
close friends is infiltrated by kneeling in church, an old-fashioned dance hall,
sculpted chocolate roses, and a fifteen-person wedding party.

But these brides can't be blamed, can't help themselves really
when they press noses against store windows and see elegant white dresses
with empire waists and velcro trains and scented veils—
the modern woman will not go against her *true* principles.
She simply can't do without the grilled butter escargot appetizer, gold-rimmed
plates, seasonal napkin rings and jasmine scented candles, and the speeches
which will clearly demonstrate she certainly appreciates the playful irony
of giving in to such an institution, considering the statements made
in her youth, when in university, when she didn't believe in anything.

saw his slain father, Mohamed Arbaji, in a dream/It was a god who stirred her to do the

I read the book sixteen times as a child, dreamt
my real father would arrive, rich and English,
sweep me into his arms to speak with Jesus,
and I'd understand, be taken care of.

The girl slept in an attic. Other children mocked her.
She ate leftovers and mice were her regular friends.
In the end they preened and pranced while
her real father paid no attention to their fancy dress.

He saw only her. The way she did the best with what
she was given. She'd become a model Christian,
despite her poverty had learned to read and write,
cook cakes and stews, sew buttons and mend socks.

I read the book sixteen times as a child. Each time
the ending pleased me more. A lantern lit inside
my pallid heart. Each time I looked at you the father
grew dark and Indian, swept me into his arms to speak

to Vishnu, and I understood, father, no one was
coming. Underneath my pillow the book grew
a second head. In the middle of the night it leapt
off my windowsill and hasn't been heard from since.

shameful thing she did/Venuste Karasira recalls he had to 'swim in the blood' of corpses, feign-

Mother adopted me when I was nine years old.
Said the weather'd been bad and kept her away.
Father called her a liar for saying so.
But father had to go.

Father had to go.
He needed to get on the quick, get paid.
Too much time wasting around with kids and stuff.
He'd had enough.

He'd had enough. So had she.
Bought a Volkswagon for a steal and shoved me in.
Four minutes in the trunk,
I was sunk.

I was sunk.
Like treasure or a horse.
The courts couldn't decide who was worse.
Mother or Father.

Father or Mother.
To plead innocent to murder in the first degree.
Post bail
And pin the blame on me.

ing to be one himself, to survive the 1994 genocide in Rwanda/They say the road is very slip-

Once a rumour
of that sort starts
there's no stopping it.

So might as well
play the big score. Slice the
damn thing off

at the core.
There's no accounting
for taste in this land.

The snakes are fake and
our fruit imported.
She did her time

and what did she get?
A few babies
and a killer no less.

Pack lightly, dear girl.
Carry-on only. Customs
here are a bitch.

News anchors are not allowed to reveal his exact whereabouts:
although we are aware he is living somewhere in Toronto
and has been for several months, once it was decided
therapy had helped enormously to beget remorse
and drugs prescribed to decrease his serious sex drive.

Yet nymphs rally each and every week with posters
depicting the deformity of his member, tallies of encounters
in woods and alleys, and court room exhibits such as knives, horns,
scissors, a sceptre or two (for the king of kings).

Is this an example of godliness?

                                            It has always been so.

While mothers parade bastard children in front of city hall
spitting at clouds, wondering will they ever know
their *real* father

or simply hear his ankle sensor beeping
while racing hotrods into the sun
eluding authorities, forcing his clouds back into mother's dark dreams.

makes of it. Take and give. I do not begrudge you. I even urge you/Ninth Person Dies after

Consider your childhood a cramped
storage space, the seat by the window where
you wished you'd be by now, the pilot

a disembodied voice inside
the head making big decisions, big
mistakes—running, running out

of luck. You dozed off during
the movie, complained about the food,
flipped through the emergency

instructions for the fifth time that hour
because you forgot to bring a magazine.
And you will die amongst these strangers,

planted in their seats: A3
14B 250G economy class. You will
make the news as a piece of luggage,

a flight schedule, a woman in tweed
distributing blankets and gum.
Here is your marriage: the wreckage

of a confused signal, father's old reprimands
etched in shattered glass, that chum
from school you thought you'd hang

with forever can only be identified
by teeth. Broken safeties, crushed
souvenirs, smashed bottles and cigarettes

you were pleased were duty-free. This
is memory: groping in the flash
for someone's hand, the smell of shampooed

Car Plows Through California Market/Nobody is my name. My father and mother call me

hair, a cell phone with your number
on it, the black box, locked and tossed
from the scene that if investigators could

unearth it, would tell all.

Once in a while Rebecca French forgets her medication and then the truth comes out. She likes the side entrance with the revolving door close to the Coughs and Cold section. She walks straight to Prescriptions Pick Up and removes her gloves, her blonde hair curled around her flushed cheeks like a scarf, the shoplifter convex mirror above shelves of antihistamines. *I deserve love*, she tells the pharmacist, who quickly checks under "F" in the bins for this month's pills. An assistant punches in an order for the birth control patch and Rebecca slams her hand down on the register. *I deserve love*, she repeats. The total changes. The assistant shrugs and smiles in her direction.

The pharmacist staples shut the bag of pills Rebecca French once in a while forgets to take, the Information Sheet side-effects sections highlighted in yellow. *My father never loved me*, Rebecca says. The birth control lady signs her credit slip. Rebecca's pills are paid for by the government. A short man in a business suit intervenes, sets grooming products on the counter. The assistant purrs a come-again. Rebecca French makes a beeline for the revolving door, the pills she forgets to take protruding from her left coat pocket. *Neither did mine*, the birth control lady admits to no one in particular.

off to foreign countries/For few are the children who turn out to be equals of their fathers, and

on the death of your mother. He would like you to know
His own mother was very important to Him
and on Mother's Day He still remembers her by passing
a particular cloud on His way to work.

He knows you have countless questions and queries
and don't wish to wait in line but rules and procedures must
be followed by everyone or the whole system crumbles.
He hopes you understand His predicament.

Remember that time is a great healer. Try to do good works
in the interim. Suffer a bit. It couldn't hurt.
Looks good on the résumé. Volunteer. I speak for
all here when I say it is best not to dwell

on matters out of your control. You loved your
mother. Did your duty. Don't question function.
Purchase insurance. Make your payments on time.
We will call when your number comes up.

She doesn't begrudge
Him anything, barely grits her teeth
when she explains *He was the favourite*
in the family, never had to share a room
or fight for the front seat of the car,
didn't get a curfew when He started to date. Or
how lonely it was not understanding His books,
the dark letters and capitals like buildings
she passed on her way to school, the secret
handshakes of His friends, and their cool
laughter whenever she tripped on His many
toys. She can even stop tears when she
talks about the beatings she got for disobeying
or the way her mother whispered in her ear
one night that she better find herself a man
if she wanted to get out and never look
back. All this is history. Only when she wakes
to the sound of a thunderstorm is she home-
sick and scared, wanting to hold Him, knowing
He won't return any of her long distance calls.

a face so ravaged all over by tears, as it is now, since nothing is gained by indiscriminate

Kleenex, Q-Tips, a pamphlet on cancer,
A broken dish, a token clip, three packs of sugar,
Shavings and a signet ring, a photograph, a finger.

A name tag, a porn mag, an amulet in amber,
A string of pearls, a blonde curl, the belt from a sander,
Kleenex, Q-Tips, a pamphlet on cancer.

Two gold buttons off his very best blazer.
A substance not identified, leftovers from dinner.
Shavings and a signet ring, a photograph, a finger.

Black socks, harsh luck, the chilly signs of winter,
A surgical glove, mud, a hairbrush full of splinters.
Kleenex, Q-Tips, a pamphlet on cancer.

Radish seeds, a swatch of tweed, an article on manners,
A light bulb, absent love, soggy remnants of anger.
Shavings and a signet ring, a photograph, a finger.

A map of the city, a referral from a doctor,
A long list of excuses on a fancy sheet of paper.
Kleenex, Q-Tips, a pamphlet on cancer,
Shavings and a signet ring, a photograph, a finger.

sorrowing/Correspondent Charlie Rose talks to Poet Laureate Billy Collins, who's not only

The war begins. My kid has the mumps.
My husband folds laundry in the kitchen
while pouring milk into his cereal. *Turn it up*,
he yells when the President's face appears (red, white
and blue) but when I do
it's just a commercial for the six o'clock
news. *I guess nothing's progressed today*, I say, except
more bodies and loaded guns. Airport
checks and taxes. *Can I watch cartoons?*
I hear from the bedroom. *Do your homework*, I tell him,
if you have so much energy.

The walkway boasts new gravel. The porch a busted light.
At night through my window I count teenagers
making out in the park, so bold today,
even queer ones, even the ones
who don't need to do it
outside. What would they do, I wonder, if
I thrust them a bottle of wine
confessed I like to watch,
that it is all I have left when the television
turns off.

My kid hides comics between the sheets.
My husband deposits the mortgage cheque.
Our air is not full of smoke or blood
or puke. Yet my sister screams
every time she spots a plane.

The war begun. Dinner is ham,
scalloped potatoes, green beans. The girl
with pierced nipples has a soaked
shirt on: my hands already
on top of her like that boy's. Anxious
to get inside.

In six months if we are still alive
I will publish this poem as a token of good will.

becoming famous, but also getting rich by writing poetry/They all would find death was quick

Suitors believe the mind does not
betray the sword, but when duped
grow desperate.

Night and day, his plans to stay thwarted
by porch, marketplace, dining hall.
Detectives sought divulgence.

One man's absence is another woman's life.
I did not think I was alive
at all. My drawers dusted

of their true calling.
Diaries problematically subjective—the words selective
to suggest an intended reader.

I knew this as my chance for freedom.
No mistakes. My ships must go.
My maids await.

Arrange pillows artfully for discovery
at daybreak. Three thousand years, I'm still unavenged.
The idiots keep up their babble.

and marriage a painful matter/Streisand claims the photos violate her right to privacy

AND BACK TO YOU ...

And Back To You And Back To You And Back To You And Back To You And Back To You

I am leaving you. Stop.
Pick up your things. Stop.
Including this. Stop.

No difference does it make, this Saturday, if love
was once in the cards. It makes no difference
to the world's economy or whether confetti will be
thrown at the horizon.

Keep up appearances, I say. Rise again. Don't
let us down. Loneliness
is much easier to assign one's self
when people expect it of you.

Dinner for one. A documentary film
on gun control. A nightcap
and a bath. Petty details

like loving. Eaten. Left. Eaten.
Regretted over again.

Do you feel the back of your hand?
It's had enough with me today. The prisons
filled with love letters
the dance halls empty.

I've got my passport stamped: Borderline.
My birth certificate: Incomplete.

I must dispel rumours of your return.

Haven't you heard?
Those who deserve love
know it, and repulse everyone.

promised to make me an immortal and all my days to be ageless but never so could she win over

Your father was right. You shouldn't have eloped
in the middle of the night. It wasn't fair.
He brought you up better than that.

Hours he toyed in your room with games and sweets spread out
on your bed: chocolate drinks, spinning tops
and needlepoint, feathers and ink

that fathered
the sonnets (even from the Portuguese). He thought
you were playing, having fun,
conjuring up a lover because
deep down he didn't think any man would see past
your condition.

He tended your flowers. Watered your
lips. Lifted each leg and arm and cleaned with the softest of cloths.

You held your head high for his benefit. Kept
your secrets intact. Stitched elms and nightingales and hoped for death.

Now, another time, another era. You think no one
would be surprised or care. But my father is

like you in his prison of a bed. With his games and treats
and children at his feet. "She should have been thinking
of another world," he wrote when he heard you'd gone.

We too will think
him a traitor when he steals away, his ladder
out of sight. Though the groom
has taken his vows and is entitled to peek: black jacket

dry cleaned, shirts pressed, limbs fastened on the blankets
like the darkest corsage.

the heart within me/A former Prime Minister says women who don't have children shouldn't

In 1992 Social Services
sent a worker to the household of Agamemnon.

Neighbour reports included
a shady character hanging around
the area, drastic changes in the children,
an overheard domestic situation and
digging in the garden at odd hours.

Time to get to the bottom of things,
the public decided. To intervene.
Despite the fact that the suspect
is a general and celebrated war hero.
The safety of children is at stake.

Too late. Agamemnon's lawyer already advised
him to burn the tapes, reconcile
with his wife and drag the daughter's
duff down the stairwell, plop
her on the chesterfield and paint a smile
on her charred lips.

The media sucked it up
like hot air. Agamemnon got fat
and found a mistress. The government
awarded him a hefty pension. The children
became the banquet at his funeral.

Everyone ate until they puked. Picked
up their coats and umbrellas and stumbled into the bloody hot night.

get pensions. A senior ruling party lawmaker suggests gang rapes are 'normal' behaviour/You

frighten me. In the waiting room
I have zero trust in the breakthroughs
of modern science, advanced stem-cell research
or drug-testing triumphs. I have two arms

and two legs, and should consider myself lucky,
but I don't. I won't be easy to deal with, the receptionist
has already gathered. I've got a bad attitude, did not fill out
the new-patient form properly, am not

sitting quietly admiring other people's children
and the William Wegman photos, pamphlets
with percentages and product reports:
Anxiety, one says,

It's Not Just in Your Head. Neither are a few hundred things
racing through my mind, including
the possibility that a clean bill
of health could be a mistake, the doctor might miss

something. *60 Minutes* is full of such reports. We write
letters, protest, but it is impossible to chart
the endless ways a body betrays. I can't even trust my vagina

not to catch something going around. And I'm bloody
careful. Do not fit any risk categories. But each year
I still spread 'em for examination.

A million people are going to get the flu shot.
A million people are going to drop dead today.
So forgive me if I don't feel calm,
if I won't unflex my fist.

should not go on clinging to your childhood. You are no longer of an age to do that/The Point is

Time you opened this:

You were never my favourite, so I didn't expect
much. Just the courtesy of our being
related and a smidgen of gratitude
for the time I wired you money
when you lost your job,
or the kids I found
after the wife
tested infertile.

I've been keeping track of the number of instances
you have written, called, or sent gifts
by mail or personal delivery
over the years (especially the last ones,
as I've been ill, you know).

These are trifling matters but the sort that constitute
character. You get this from
your mother, you understand.
From your father, you get
my deal-with-it
attitude. I'm not
sure I should've
had you.

But I did.
Now I will deal with it.
Deal with you.

Time you read this:

If you live under my roof, you
live by my rules: be thankful
for anything you get, love when it
is not useful to love, divide your
heart equally amongst
family. Pray.

Rehabilitation/I am not being proud, nor indifferent, nor puzzled beyond need/China's ambi-

The gates are closing.
Your mailbox jammed with lies.

If you thought living had too many conditions,
just wait till you die.

tious economic growth plans are environmentally unachievable because the world does not

When Zeus gets that funky feeling he could rent a "Girls Girls Girls"
video, sip on a slurpee, and purchase a new suit. Persephone,
dressed to the nines in killer boots, her mother could whisk her
to a photo booth, four pics for three dollars, and no sorrowful
parting during business hours would be tolerated.

Something has to replace the terror.
Something shiny and air conditioned, with escalators
and stands of affordable jewellery from Spain or Mexico.
Abandon your boats, treasure-hunters.
There's enough fast food to stock a million ships.

And let's not forget shoes. Shoes for all the ladies.
Buy one get one free!
Shoes for all that running and crawling. A fragrant foot
cream and pumice stone for calluses and sores.

Get a perm. A fur coat. DVD. Lawnmower.
Plan an Alaskan cruise.

Get contacts blue as the ocean. Go on.
No one believes that nonsense about sacrifice anymore. Altars
display the latest in kitchen ware.
No one cares

if you can't afford it. Apply for credit. Miles and miles of credit.
Sleep soundly in king-sized beds. Do-not-pay-
a-cent. Your children's children
and their children's children
can waste their own lives
paying it off.

have enough resources to allow its 1.3 billion people to become Western-style consumers/She

She thinks this might be the place
to settle down, despite the obvious danger.

Time to hang up her belt. Let anger
subside. Accept the inner peace of mountain ranges.
The scorpion in its waning seconds.

Two world titles, among many others. Was it imperative
to prove one's self again? She'd thought so,
but times change. A woman gets
lonely, starts to want
friends, a family.

Beneath the rubble
Bellona pulls out her groom.
Drops her checkered skirt over the sky.

cries high and shrill, while the men behind her, hitting her with their spear butts on the back

God takes her guard down on sunny days,
watches from the crust of road.
It's Tuesday, the day
of liquid. It drips.

Skin helpless. She has no screen.
"Come back," she screams, heels digging
in the dirt. The patrol car gurgles. "Can't you see
a young lady needs a lift?"

"Eternity or Bust," she reads
on the bumper and curdles.
The same man beat her with his belt
last Tuesday, fucked her
up the ass twice. Kept
saying she was *too naughty*
to be out alone.

There's no joy in sunshine.
Blisters rise, burst. Her black eye
is closing. It hurts more
than Saturday or Sunday because
you expect bad things
to happen to good people
when it rains.

Expect her to stay stranded
until the end of time.
It's sunny. The ditches are dry.

and the shoulders, force her up and lead her away into slavery to have hard work and sor-

There is another woman
in my apartment. I'm sure of it.

She tosses my stockings around.
Signs my chequebook.
Sings god-awful songs
in the shower.

Sometimes I don't think I mind her:
when she tells the telemarketers
to fuck off, or pretends
to be the lady of the house
when politicians stop by
for tea or leaves
short love-notes
in my packed lunch.

There must be another woman
in my apartment
who can play the piano, drop
and do fifty, snap
into a tantrum on the turn
of a dime.

She's tempestuous, tempting.
Her rages. Her fires.
Once inside my body

she will sprout strong teeth.
Eat me out and take over
completely. My skull

a cockpit. My eyes held hostage.

row/Rabbi gets Life in Prison, Still Professes Innocence in Wife's Slaying/Your heart was

Love is a distraction. Something to do between the crib
and cultivating new nations. In fact, it's so distracting you can surprise
lovers out on a stroll in the woods or making beds
by your eyes alone. Funny how they get when they know
you've been watching, keeping track
of hotel visits, girdles, and other gifts offered
in moments of passion, sultry whispers and excuses
to wives. Make up your mind lovers. Either
you want no one or all to take notice. You
can't have both. Love is having one's cake
and eating it until you're sick—until you wish
you could purge but you don't want anyone else
to injest it. Most importantly, for myths to work, lovers
must be unmoved that suffering surrounds them. Obliviousness
is key. To the heart. The nervous system. The gregarious garden
and its triumph of trees and birds—all lovers
lost by looking around.

My father fell out of his wheelchair again
and when the ambulance attendants arrived they hoisted him up
like a band of logs (legs splintered

arms like
abandoned wings of windmills) he told them not to
take him to the hospital unless they wanted

him to die. His homemaker would punch in
at ten to turn him on his side and
there was the news at eleven he felt

he should keep up on and maybe his son or daughter
would call and ask how he'd been coping
with the new pills. But

they didn't and I only found out what happened
when the nurse said he'd been
released.

not a good quality/Is the Weather Fast Enough for You?/Why did you ask me that? You should

—Is there a God?

—If we invent one.

—Do you want to invent one?

—I might if it served a purpose.

—Could there be a purpose?

—Only if people would no longer suffer.

—Would people no longer suffer?

—It's hard to tell. It's never been tried before.

—But there have been gods before.

—Surely.

—Then there have been attempts before.

—Not to erase suffering.

—Then to erase what?

—Mothers, fathers, babies. That kind of thing.

—What do the gods want with them?

—Worship.

—What is worship?

—Anything that is not you.

—Is it good for the gods?

not learn it, nor know what my mind knows/A giant catfish that ate a dog and terrorized a

—Oh, yes. But bad for you.

—Because I will suffer.

—Yes.

—Unless I worship?

—Unless you are worshipped.

—But shouldn't it be a two-way street?

—No. An alleyway will do.

—Can I have my own name?

—Yes, it won't change anything.

—Can I have someone to speak to?

—It won't change anything.

—Can I have a heart?

—It won't change anything.

—How about you?

—Me? I have no questions.

—Then you must be a god.

—Then you must suffer.

German lake for years is dead/I am no prophet, nor do I know the ways of birds clearly/

THE MAN ON THE STREET ...

Women invented hoof-and-mouth disease
according to Homer and Euripedes.

Women need meat to fill their dreams.

For life is brutal,
but sleep,
    sleep,
     sleep,
       is a massacre.

Do you agree with British Prime Minister Blair that 'history will forgive' the war in Iraq

Foreign media are experiencing difficulty
infiltrating the borders set by soldiers. We hope to have
a moving picture or at least a sound bite soon.
Please stay tuned.

Troy is impossible country in which to stage a war.
Language problems persist. Religious faux-pas
have escalated tensions on both sides.

We will stay on location
until this conflict works itself to a conclusion.
We await a heads-up from Homer.
Though he can be tricky, asks for money,
he's the best informant we've got right now.

Rest assured,
we will not leave these hills, have packed
loads of batteries. We will feed you
a line when one becomes available. Until
then read maps, locate
leaders in their caves. Pick
a side to cheer for.

Then clear your plates.
There will be much to stomach at once.

even though Saddam Hussein posed no immediate threat? ✔ *yes or* ✔ *no/Teiresias the*

Pierre Savoie's letter (Nov. 16)
really brought to light a number of things
that are misrepresented in the media. But, let us not
stop at religious claims.

I am tired of this newspaper
presenting scientific theories as truths. I cannot
count the number of times I have heard
about "atoms" and "gravity" as if
they had been proven to exist. Speaking

of existence, that is only a theory. In the future,
please add the words "alleged" or "believed to be"
before people's names, since there are people
in the world who do not believe
that anyone exists.

Your newspaper should respect
the varying views of the populace, and admit
that even the world itself could be no more
than something I am currently dreaming.

Theben, the blind prophet, whose senses stay unshaken within him, to whom alone Persephone

It feels nice to say the words:
gardenia, daffodil, tiger lily,
or *petunia*. But other words
are pretty too: *dysentery, cancer,*
diphtheria, Alzheimer's;
they just have bad associations.
A major disease of trees
and shrubs is *honey fungus*.
None will cure. What's in a name?

Whether or not the blue whale
survives will not ensure world
peace or save the woman
down the street from phoning
with another *domestic*.

Mother bird kicked
baby out because
she didn't want to share a worm.
Nature does not adhere
to affirmative action.

The child and the ripped tulip
pressed in his palm do not
last. Do not mean more than:
here. The sea drowns
as much as it saves.

Sometimes I'm not sure I agree with what I write,
if the air I breathe is really and truly stale and bland
in the basement. If you have a pointed nose
like a bird's beak or eyes the shade of burnt sunflowers.
I'm at a loss as to whether our house has Victorian trim
around the windows or an art-deco kitchen, and no one's
confirmed to my satisfaction that the door handle
jiggles because of that awful winter in 1995.

Is my father actually to be pitied?
My mother mythologized?
My version of my lost childhood anthologized?

I've got the sad thing down like a posture.
The weeping willows roll in when called.
Death warrants stack themselves paper upon
paper, never caught in the printer.

Sorrow is no longer unexpected. It arrives
with every breath and bird's beak and door handle. Winter
or summer, that awful feeling of it being here
whether it's already left or not.

Health Organization declared yesterday that SARS can be contained around the world/I

Sebastian thinks a black hole is something you poke sticks in.

Measurements impossible to calculate
because instruments get stuck
and there's no way to draw them back—

not with fishing line or nylon rope
or a ten dollar bill. Pilot projects remain
lost in space with debris and rock flakes
and galaxies. Light cannot penetrate
where it forays, crushed into submission.

Sebastian was reading about it in his science textbook.

Black holes can be photographed. They can be named
and discovered. But you need to be careful
approaching one. It does not like you. Or
it says it does, and then you don't like it.

The pages ripped out are wet, an entire section smeared.
A roast turns on the campfire. The smoke
from the scout leader's cigarette drifts exactly
to his tent

> —came up with the term to reflect
> its immensity—

tucks in the hollow of his sleeping bag.
He makes his mind dark. His legs and thighs darker.
The hair sprouting in his armpits he imagines
as light years away. There is no safe touching.

admire you and wonder, and am terribly afraid to clasp you by the knees/Ground shook as oak

The feast begins and the speeches.
We should all be doing our part,
reminds the MP. We have a duty
to those less fortunate than ourselves,
waves the Sunshine Girl to the film producer.
We're living in a time of serious crisis,
ponders the public intellectual.

The line-up starts to the left and curls right
like a long snake in the grass, rattling without speaking.

More and more, they trudge through the door,
after cameras have left, but the two hour shift
not yet completed. The anchorman asks
his agent for a cola. The head of the branch plant
complains his feet ache, secretly
thankful they only sponsor this occasion
once a year.

The hunger fed.
The hunger surfaced.
The many, many pairs of panning hands.

The only time plenty has made them nervous.

A Thousand Fishes, A Thousand Loaves.

My God, there's enough here to feed an army,
the Mayor exclaims.

Exactly.

topples/Unhappy men, who went alive to the house of Hades, so dying twice, when all the rest

The book is an artifact, its dusty
leaves like layers of desert sand.

Bindings cannot stand the competition,
the glittering lights, graphic

flashiness of electric communication.
Take this ache and make it a web-page

this joy and make it an emoticon. Upon
the screen masses edit elaborate memorials.

Metaphor is dead. The poet a recycled
identity. Hold the Enter key to your lips

and press. Page Up, Page Down, Insert
Symbol, Control. Alt. Delete. Privately

a new generation of readers is busy
restructuring old verse, cutting out tongues.

The ultimate translation project:
The Word is already obsolete.

One more reason to turn:
Time's face is yours:

century of numbers. Overrated
heads. Like tongues
and husbands, I have been hiding

out in bunkers since I was electrified.
Midnight we switch sides:
children drift asleep in ashes,

organize fire drills. I took
the railroad here. The cars packed,
I latched onto the side

like a spider on a web. Someone's
lunch. Another woman who shouldn't
be travelling after dark.

Shhh! The secret service is knocking.
They say I've forged my papers.

Time goes on:
Clutches and chokes.
Into the mouths of babes spits sand.

small groups into the larger populace/It is my fate to be a wanderer among men. Give me a

Scenes considered too disturbing,
too vivid for delicate tastes. So
pan the planes, the fire bombs,
answering machine messages full

of final seconds of clarity. *Just like a
movie, just like a movie.* The general
public enjoys a good movie. But destroy
documentation of those who pushed

the epileptic down the stairs, who jumped
in front of a baby stroller to safety,
the cut-throat businessmen ordering
disciplinary action to anyone who left

the meeting before it was *absolutely
necessary.* Palestinian mourners offering
mangoes to families at the American
embassy. Cut that. Pull the tape of Pakistani

peasants gathering clothes and bandages
to send over. Organize a panel of religious
leaders and cue the violin behind the Christian,
the Jew, the Buddhist monk, the Muslim cleric

place in your ship/Brokaw: But isn't that a failure of intelligence to some degree? Brener: No, I

while the Pentagon sizzles in the
background. Select files of known terrorists,
publish their names. But don't release photos
of dinner tables stationed like wedding

guests each with a number corresponding to
a floor. How most strode over and witnessed
best friend, brother, mother, child pass on
to deceased from the missing person list.

Don't let us inside a woman's purse who's
written to her lover grounded in Tokyo. *I work
with goddamn Muslims. Come for me soon.*
The tens of thousands of dollars offered

for film footage of the towers tumbling down.
Blood transfusions. Severed limbs.
Students at the university who don't want to study
the Holocaust. *Even if it did happen,* they tell me,
what's the point, you can't prove it.

don't get into the argument about intelligence or not. What different would have been done? I'd

They must be tasty.
Go well with potatoes and pasta
or red beets and cranberry relish.
Hot or cold. Boiled or roasted. Peeled
or whole. There must be vitamins
and nutrients found in no other flesh.
A chemical release like that
of seratonin. I'm sure the giblets
are excellent for soup.

Children as boxed lunches or
TV dinners. Children as midnight
snacks. Craved like pickles
when you're pregnant,
licorice at the movies. Someone
ought to package them as eggs,
twelve to a carton.
Many look enough alike.

Stores should stock them
at cash registers, coin
dispensers in washrooms.
You can never tell when
the urge might hit you.

Children's Aid says it's an epidemic.
Kings and Queens, mad Titans
are not the only ones with
peculiar palates. Their parents
just couldn't wait to spit
or shit them out.

still have the same problem/Bring us beautiful victims/Spot Checks Would be Implemented in

leave your weapons
these women sprint quicker than lightning
denser than oak
and though drawn young and limber
are old and flabby
and have lost their hair

no one has their number
when they run (forget tricks
like flinging rocks, beyond
distraction—that was just a letter-to-the-editor
written by a few sore losers
after the boars' heads were hoisted high)

thickets thicken
and foliage foils

my mother told me when nymphs
lose their pride
they shed skin and become
bashful boys

who can't bear to pitch tents without a tale
or two

the warm flesh
of imaginations
turning on a spit

the bush of the forest
brown
roasting fire

planets reunite and old lovers
decide to give it a rest
for once

the sounds and sights of childhood
slide off watchtowers
and town clocks

patients condense as unlit candles

father forgives himself

the morning glory whispers to you
in the most exquisite foreign language
you've ever dreamed of learning

priests hold their tongues
and read Harlequin romances
and Choose-Your-Own-Adventure

teenage girls head home
in packs

the shy streetcar conductor
rehearses his lines
a trumpet wakes the cleaning crew

no one wants to go
but the police have arrived

and statues burn with flags of all nations
trapped like children
in car-seats

going over the side

time to come if you kill the singer of songs/Whereabouts of 12 year-old still unknown although

The instructor advises to take authority seriously.
Try to identify sources
of anger to construct reasonable solutions.

Giving it a go, is Athena. She wants balance
and grace to match her wisdom. *I have frequently
thought of suicide, but of course for me
it isn't an option*, she noted on her questionnaire.
Though I would like to die someday.

Hera has an eating disorder. Charybdis refuses
to share a room. Diana just
can't take the responsibility. *So tired,
no thanks in this line of work anymore.*

Zeus sits sulking in the corner. This is by court order.
*I'll sue every one of you fucking
bastards, as soon as my lawyer
busts me from this place.* Orderlies load
his tranquilizers.

There are always more women here than men.
More mothers than single gals.
More programs than people.

Take classes and medicines. Take
charge of personal demons. Make
peace with the body. Make
peace with your god.

Philomela, a permanent patient, excels
at expressive dance. Swaying like a sail
upon the waters, you can almost believe
she's reaching distant lands of such wonder
her arms and mouth were sent to prepare
for her arrival in advance.

she phoned home late Tuesday to say she was safe/They struggled with their feet for a little,

Forget Greece this summer and Tel Aviv this winter.
Forget Rome or Paris or Cleveland. Forget your doctor's appointment
and your niece's sweet sixteen. Your lunch on Tuesday with the girls,
your high-school reunion. Your neighbour's name. Forget the hairdryer
and the seven-in-one miracle appliance. The television or the radio.
Forget you forgot to use the radio in years. Forget it.

Blocked by the sun. The shadow
is a second bruise around the eye.
In the west, on drunken evenings, I beg. Turn,
let me see if you're hurt.

I did not intend to discuss Religion today
or have any thoughts
beyond the morning sun. But so be it.
I am hungry at this hour
and it's as good a reason as any
to be somewhat in the philosophical frame of mind.

That was the book I was saving
for a pleasant afternoon with the cat and a cup of tea.
I had no intention of taking it down
and tearing out the pages
before reading them. No drive towards destruction
when I first awoke and noticed that
most of my life is missing
and I never got to say goodbye.

I hope the me teetering at the edge of the world
is dancing, that she has learned how to unfold
her arms and accept enlightenment, that she
will not let I Don't Know be the final
answer to the eternal Why.

I hope she has a basket of hearts
in her closet. That she chooses her sacrifice carefully
and offers it at the right time, when
she is sure there will be a morning sun
and a good book waiting for someone
and the abandoned cats in the neighbourhood are lapping
up the milk dripping
off her coat.

years ago over a pack of smokes/It is not good to go on mourning forever/One of Elvis Presley's

twisted into the roots
of the tree,

twisted into the roots
of the tree,

twisted into the roots
of the tree,

the tree,

the tree,

the tree,

the tree,

she died.

teeth is on the auction block along with a lock of his hair and one of his gold records/But

Slip under the door
and I will help you tie
the square knot your father taught you
on your last camping trip
that you've forgotten.

On the far left wall
is a portrait of a piano.
Take three steps back
and fine handwriting will appear--
a note from your first love
wishing to hear how you sound.

Open the cupboards in the kitchen
and in every cracker box and soup can
filled to the brim
is all the loose change you've
ever lost or given away.

Lift the duvet in the bedroom.
There lies the word on the tip of your tongue
the scent of your mother's hair
the bright bell of a happy new year.

The lights wane, but I am floating
like a feather above you. Lie down.
Stay awhile. Please. Let yourself
be led to believe that every so often
good things happen.

Rumor, a messenger, went swiftly through all the city/ Sleep is oblivion of all things, both good

Blinded by the heat, I keep track of the humidity factor:
barometers fix actual temperature, but according to meteorologists
It will feel a whole lot hotter

if science is able to separate fields of space
in this summer wave
why shouldn't we

I bring you my childhood traumas on a serving tray
and you can say, *They aren't so bad,* and I will admit the facts, but
It feels like abuse of the worst kind

I wonder if Einstein predicted this warping
of his theory of relativity
as it did for light and dice: how there must be a plan
to all solid bodies, all forces of attraction
repulsion families brought together through magnetism

propelled and patronized by physics:
and it will be the end of the world as it races towards its final state
but it very well might feel like a miraculous beginning

and evil, when it has shrouded the eyelids/ Israel may free extremists, latest report says/

BREAKING NEWS ...

You would not know it:
thirty seconds after foam
collects at the bottom
of the cup: I strap myself
in: lift the latch and hang
on tight: cross the street
in my Trojan horse.

It used to be that kids played outside until the street lamps came on. But not anymore. With

I don't know why. I've never been.
I'm not especially fond of Oriental films, Oriental art or customs.
I'm not even sure I could stand the heat.

But sometimes I think I would like to die in the Orient
because there live a billion people and I want to be
buried among them, perhaps learn to appreciate
eastern culture in death. A few words
in dialect and maybe heaven will be different.

Not like what's promised here. I don't want that heaven.
Don't want to be a part of it. I've escaped
my whole life. Please, don't let me escape
my death.

Let me feel as lost
and sorry and scared
as a kidnapped tourist.

Push me down to my knees
in overpopulated streets. Empty my pockets.
Paint on my body a pattern I have yet to discover
in my *Book of World Myths and Religions*.

Give me just a moment of your time.
I'll find some room for this long, slow flight
to oblivion. I promise, you won't even notice I'm here.

the abduction and murder of Holly Jones looming large in most parents' minds, parents are

for all the Greek ladies raped in the first two hundred pages alone
of Ovid's *Metamorphoses*, not that I'm in favour of censorship
or rewriting history to ease disturbed sleep
but I have a feeling these events really did transpire as told
and I'm supposed to know and *do* something.

Isn't that why the dead come back—to force us to act? If not, should
I be fascinated by the legion of illegitimate children Jove fostered
unaware they were his? Am I requisitioned to recover
a lost will or secret stash? Open a charity or draft
a petition in the names of these children

comfort their mothers from this land: there is no rape here sweet Proserpina,
you will not be ravaged. I can't exactly lie to the dead. That would be worse
than doing nothing, don't you think? But what have we got here: shelters;
and since I'm no inventor I suppose I could build one between pages 76 and 77
and all the nymphs could hide there, escorted by Diana

but only after being raped
after they are no longer virgins
and maybe that's why I'm not in favour of rewriting history and will
finish the book, and turn into an eagle or snake or a mad ocean goddess
in grief for having thought so

keeping children close by, and their children are facing a difficult and strange isolation/

So let us go on a washing tomorrow...

It is hateful to me
to tell a story over again, when it has been well told.

This book is also dedicated to

Samantha Zacher for

being here

&

Jit Uppal
my brother

About the Cover: I first saw Leonor Fini's *L'ombrelle* at The Metropolitan Museum of Art in New York City in May 2002 when it was featured as part of the *Surrealism: desire unbound* exhibition. It has been reproduced by kind permission of the Trustees of the Edward James Foundation, West Dean Estate, Chichester, England and the Estate of Leonor Fini. Special thanks to Richard Overstreet at the Estate, Sharon-Michi Kusunoki at the Foundation, and Neil Zuckerman at the CFM Gallery in New York who helped me track the painting down.

About the Text: *Live Coverage*'s news crawl is composed of lines from Richmond Lattimore's translation of Homer's *The Odyssey* and headlines from various print and on-line sources including *Time, Chatelaine, CNN, Hollywood Online, CBC, MSNBC, Canada AM, 60 Minutes, ABC News, The Globe and Mail, The National Post,* and *The Toronto Star.* The lines from *The Odyssey* have been reproduced by kind permission of HarperCollins US.

"Now You Don't Have to Follow the News, the News Follows You" is a found poem also composed of headlines from the above news sources. "Media Misrepresentation Doesn't Stop at Religion" is a found poem from the letters-to-the-editor section of Toronto's *MetroToday* on Wednesday, November 14, 2001.

Thank you to all those people who helped with this project: Richard Teleky, for always being there to read poems and answer the phone and discuss just about everything; Tim Hanna for bringing to this design idea his unending enthusiasm and loyalty and a willingness to work with me and experiment at every stage of the process; Christian Bök for insightful and helpful suggestions; Barry Callaghan, for being much more than a publisher, being proud; Samantha Zacher, a home away from home for me too; Jit Uppal, for taking care of the future; Avtar Uppal, for the files; and all other friends and family for your love and support.

Thanks as well to the editors and publishers who have supported me and/or published my work since the last collection. Thanks in particular to *Body Language: A Head-to-Toe Anthology, Exile—the Literary Quarterly, The Fiddlehead, The Globe and Mail, Grain, Intangible, The Neubaucher Gallery, Pagitica, Tessera* and *Universe*. Sections of this book were also delivered as part of a lecture entitled "News that Stays News: Revisionist Mythmaking in the 21st Century" for the Vanier College Fellows Lecture Series, York University. Thanks to York University and the Humanities Division for welcoming me into the fold.

Lastly, all my love and gratitude to Christopher Doda. Thank you. You are with me with every word.